Sous Vide Recipes

Quick and Easy Sous Vide Recipes

for Everyone!

John Peters

Table of Contents

Chapter One: What Do You Need for Sous Vide?

Different Sous Vide Machines

Sous vide equipment has been around for decades and is quite popular in professional kitchens. This piece of equipment was rather expensive, bulky, and came with plenty of complicated features. However, with increasing awareness about this popular method of cooking, several sous vide machines were introduced to the consumer market. In this section, let us look at some of the basic types of equipment you can consider while building your very own sous vide setup at home!

Immersion Circulator

An immersion circulator is a kitchen tool that heats water and then circulates it around in the pot while maintaining an even yet precise temperature. Immersion circulators are quite affordable, making these the most popular sous vide machine options today. Since they don't have an inbuilt water bath, they don't take up much space. A standalone device doesn't require any additional equipment, since it can be easily clamped on and adjusted to suit to the pots you use. Some of the best sous vide immersion circulators include the Anova Precision Cooker, Nomiku, ChefSteps Joule, and Sansaire.

Sous Vide Water Oven

The sous vide water oven is a countertop water bath. These are generally the same size as a microwave and are fully contained sous vide devices. A basic sous vide water oven costs at least $500. This device heats water but doesn't circulate it the way an immersion cooker does, which might result in certain inconsistencies while cooking and in the resultant textures, too. AquaChef, Gourmia, and SousVide Supreme are some examples of water ovens. The Instant Pot and other multi-use cookers like Gourmia and Oliso offer sous vide capabilities.

If you're hesitant about investing in a sous vide device right now, then you might want to try DIY sous vide hacks. If you have a rice cooker or a slow cooker at home, you can try a sous vide recipe using a reusable silicone bag that's immersed in water. The results won't be as consistent as what you would see with an immersion cooker, but you will get an idea of how sous vide works.

Sous Vide Packaging

The packaging is an important aspect of sous vide cooking. When food is sealed in containers or bags appropriate for sous vide, these will prevent evaporation while increasing the efficiency of the cooking process. Place all the ingredients as per the recipe in a plastic bag and remove all air present within using a vacuum sealer, immersion technique, or even a straw. You don't even need to invest in a vacuum sealer. Some of the packaging options available include vacuum-sealing bags, resealable bags (like Ziploc's freezer-safe bags), reusable silicone bags, and canning jars.

How to Use Sous Vide?

Sous vide is indeed quite a simple technique, but getting it right does take some practice. In this section, we will learn some tips that will come in handy while using a sous vide machine.

Before you place an ingredient in the pouch, ensure that you have seasoned it thoroughly. While seasoning, however, keep in mind that certain herbs and spices can become overpowering or even go rancid when cooked for extended periods, like garlic, onion greens, pepper, rosemary, thyme, and cumin. Even fresh herbs can lose their original flavor during sous vide cooking, and therefore it is always better to season ingredients with dried herbs.

When the water begins circulating in the water bath, it will eventually start to evaporate. Water will evaporate when it is in constant contact with direct heat for extended periods. Vapor will start gathering within the sous vide machine, which will reduce the level of water in the bath and might even damage the sous vide equipment. If the water level falls, then the cooking process will also be affected. To prevent this, cover the water bath with plastic wrap. This also reduces the chances of heat escaping.

Before you place the bag in the water bath, ensure that it has been vacuum-sealed properly. If there are any air pockets present in the bag, then the resultant dish will not be evenly cooked. The simplest way to check this is by ensuring that the bag is directly in contact with all the ingredients placed within.

The bag can be popped up or down or even shifted above the surface in a circulator. If the bag is properly vacuum-sealed, then it will generally stay submerged. It also depends on the weight of the ingredients you use. If you're cooking an ingredient like fish, the circulator might end up pushing the ingredients around the water bath. Adding any food-safe weights to the vacuum bag is the best way to ensure it always remains submerged.

Perhaps the best way to cook red meat is sous vide. This not only helps retain the natural textures and flavors present in the meat, but also enhances its flavor profile. If you want to extract more flavor from the meat, then always slightly sear your cuts in a pan before vacuum sealing. Alternately, you can also sear the meat after it has cooked in the water bath. Since the bag is vacuum-sealed, all the natural juices will stay contained in the meat. The meat will also start cooking in its own juices, and the residual fats or juices can be used to make a jus to serve on the side.

If you like the idea of cooking juicy and moist chicken every single time, then try sous vide. Cooking chicken at high temperatures ends up charring the external surface while leaving it raw in the middle. When cooked directly on heat, the chances of overcooking the chicken also increase. To avoid all this, opt for sous vide. Once you remove the chicken from the sous vide pouch, sear it on a sizzling hot pan for a couple of seconds. The same technique can be used for cooking pork.

Temperature for Different Meats

Ribeye, Porterhouse, and Strip Steaks

COOK	TEMPERATURE	TIME
Very rare to rare	120°F to 128°F	1 to 2 ½ hours
Medium-rare	129°F to 134°F	1 to 4 hours
Medium	135°F to 144°F	1 to 4 hours
Medium-well	145°F to 155°F	1 to 3 hours
Well done	156°F	1 to 3 hours

Hamburgers

COOK	TEMPERATURE	TIME
Very rare to rare	115°F to 123°F	40 minutes to 2 ½ hours
Medium-rare	124°F to 129°F	40 minutes to 2 ½ hours
Medium	130°F to 137°F	40 minutes to 4 hours
Medium-well	138°F to 144°F	40 minutes to 4 hours
Well done	145°F to 155°F	40 minutes to 3 ½ hours

Tenderloin Steaks

COOK	TEMPERATURE	TIME
Very rare to rare	120°F to 128°F	45 minutes to 2 ½ hours
Medium-rare	129°F to 134°F	45 minutes to 4 hours
Medium	135°F to 144°F	45 minutes to 4 hours
Medium-well	145°F to 155°F	45 minutes to 3 ½ hours
Well done	156°F	1 to 3 hours

Chicken Breasts

COOK	TEMPERATURE	TIME
Tender and juicy (cold salads)	150°F	1 to 4 hours
Very soft and juicy (serve hot)	140°F	1 ½ to 4 hours
Juicy, tender, and a little stringy (serve hot)	150°F	1 to 4 hours
Traditional: juicy, firm, slightly stringy (serve hot)	160°F	1 to 3 hours

Chicken Thighs

COOK	TEMPERATURE	TIME
Firm, juicy, and a little tough	150°F	1 to 4 hours
Tender and very juicy	165°F	1 to 4 hours
Falls-off-the-bone tender	165°F	4 to 8 hours

Pork Chops and Roast

COOK	TEMPERATURE	TIME
Rare	136°F	1 to 3 hours
Medium-rare	144°F	1 to 3 hours
Well done	158°F	1 to 3 hours

Tough Cuts of Pork

COOK	TEMPERATURE	TIME
Rare	140°F	8 to 24 hours
Medium-rare	154°F	8 to 24 hours
Well done	185°F	8 to 24 hours

Pork Ribs

COOK	TEMPERATURE	TIME
Succulent, tender, and meaty	145°F	36 hours
Traditional BBQ	165°F	12 hours

Fish

COOK	TEMPERATURE	TIME
Tender	104°F	40 to 70 minutes
Tender and flaky	122°F	40 to 70 minutes
Well done	131°F	40 to 70 minutes

Vegetables

TYPE	TEMPERATURE	TIME
Green vegetables	180°F	10 to 20 minutes
Root vegetables	185°F	10 to 20 minutes
Winter squash	185°F	10 to 20 minutes

Fruits

TYPE	TEMPERATURE	TIME
Warm and ripe	154°F	1 ¾ hour to 2 ½ hours
Cooked soft (ideal for purees)	185°F	30 minutes to 1 ½ hours

Chapter Two: Sous Vide Jams and Preserves

Bourbon-Maple Chutney

Serves: 15 or 16

Ingredients:

- 2 Braeburn apples or any other baking apples, peeled, cored, diced

- 4 tablespoons maple syrup

- 2 tablespoons lemon juice

- 1 teaspoon chipotle chili powder

- 6 tablespoons bourbon

- 2 tablespoons minced thyme leaves

- 2 tablespoons melted butter

- Salt to taste

- Pepper to taste

Directions:

1. Follow the instructions given in the manual and fill the sous vide water oven. Preheat it to 185°F.

2. Add apples into a large vacuum-seal pouch or Ziploc bag.

3. Add rest of the ingredients into a bowl and stir until well combined.

4. Pour into the pouch and vacuum seal. Shake the pouch until well combined.

5. Submerge the pouch in the water bath and set the timer for 1 ½ to 2 hours.

6. Empty the contents into an airtight container. Stir until thick and smooth. Close the container.

7. Refrigerate until use, for up to one week.

Blueberry Compote

Serves: 8 to 10

Ingredients:

- 16 ounces blueberries

- Zest of 2 oranges, grated

- Zest of 2 lemons, grated

- 2 tablespoons honey

- ¼ teaspoon ground cinnamon

Directions:

1. Follow the instructions given in the manual and fill the sous vide water oven. Preheat it to 183°F.

2. Place blueberries, honey, cinnamon, and zests in a large Ziploc bag or vacuum-seal pouch.

3. Vacuum seal the pouch and shake until well combined.

4. Submerge the pouch in the water bath and set the timer for 30 to 60 minutes.

5. When the timer goes off, remove the bag from the water bath. Empty the contents from the pouch into an airtight container. Stir until thick and smooth. Close the container.

6. Refrigerate until use, for up to 10 days.

Spicy Rhubarb Compote

Serves: 15 to 18

Ingredients:

- ½ cup honey
- 2 cups sugar
- 4 cups red wine
- 4 teaspoons red pepper flakes
- ¼ teaspoon salt
- 6 strips (2 inches each) orange peel
- 20 stalks rhubarb, trimmed, cut into 1-inch pieces
- ¼ teaspoon ground cloves (optional)
- ¼ teaspoon ground cinnamon (optional)
- ¼ teaspoon ground cardamom (optional)

Directions:

1. Follow the instructions given in the manual and fill the sous vide water oven. Preheat it to 180°F.

2. Add sugar, wine, pepper flakes, and orange flakes into a saucepan. Place the saucepan over high heat and bring to a boil. Stir frequently until sugar dissolves completely.

3. Add rhubarb and salt into a vacuum-seal pouch or Ziploc bag. Turn off the heat and pour into the pouch. Vacuum seal the pouch.

4. Submerge the pouch in the water bath and set the timer for 45 minutes, or until the stalks are tender.

5. When done, remove the pouch from the water bath. Empty the liquids from the pouch into a saucepan. Heat over medium flame and stir frequently until liquid thickens.

6. Place rhubarb in a shallow bowl. Pour the thickened syrup over the rhubarb. Cover and let it cool to room temperature.

7. Refrigerate until use, for up to one week.

Sous Vide Strawberry-Rhubarb Jam

Serves: 20 to 25

Ingredients:

- 2 cups diced strawberries

- 2 cups diced rhubarb

- 2 cups granulated sugar

- 4 tablespoons fresh lemon juice

- 4 tablespoons powdered pectin

Directions:

1. Follow the instructions given in the manual and fill the sous vide water oven. Preheat it to 180°F.

2. Add strawberries, rhubarb, sugar, lemon juice, and pectin into a large Ziploc bag or vacuum-seal pouch. Press the bag a few times so that the ingredients are well combined.

3. Vacuum seal the pouch.

4. Submerge the pouch in the water bath and set the timer for 90 minutes.

5. When done, remove the pouch from the water bath. Empty the contents of the pouch into an airtight container. Cool completely.

6. Refrigerate until use, for up to 10 days.

Sous Vide Peaches

Serves: 12

Ingredients:

- 6 pounds peaches, peeled, pitted, sliced

- 1 cup white wine

- 12 tablespoons sugar

- 8 teaspoons torn rose geranium leaves or 1 teaspoon vanilla extract or a 3-inch stick cinnamon

Directions:

1. Follow the instructions given in the manual and fill the sous vide water oven. Preheat it to 150°F.

2. Place all the ingredients in a large vacuum-seal pouch or Ziploc bag. Press the bag a few times so that the ingredients are well combined.

3. Vacuum seal the pouch.

4. Submerge the pouch in the water bath and set the timer for 45 minutes.

5. When done, remove the pouch from the water bath. Empty the contents of the pouch into an airtight container. Cool completely.

6. Refrigerate until use, for up to 10 days.

Raspberry Preserves

Serves: 12 to 15

Ingredients:

- 4 cups fresh raspberries

- 1 cup granulated sugar

- 2 teaspoons grated fresh lemon zest

- 6 tablespoons tapioca starch

- 2 teaspoons fresh lemon juice

- 2 teaspoons pure vanilla extract

Directions:

1. Follow the instructions given in the manual and fill the sous vide water oven. Preheat it to 190°F.

2. Place all the ingredients in a large vacuum-seal pouch or Ziploc bag. Press the bag a few times so that the ingredients are well combined.

3. Vacuum seal the pouch.

4. Submerge the pouch in the water bath and set the timer for 45 minutes.

5. Just before the timer goes off, make an ice water bath by filling a large bowl with water and ice.

6. When done, remove the pouch from the water bath and immerse in the ice water bath. When cooled, remove the

pouch from the water bath. Empty the contents into an airtight container.

7. Refrigerate until use, for up to 10 days.

Strawberry-Basil Maple Syrup

Serves: 20 to 25

Ingredients:

- 4 cups pure maple syrup

- 2 cups loosely-packed basil leaves

- 16 ounces strawberries, sliced

- 1 teaspoon fine sea salt

Directions:

1. Follow the instructions given in the manual and fill the sous vide water oven. Preheat it to 135°F.

2. Add all the ingredients into a vacuum-seal pouch or Ziploc bag.

3. Vacuum seal the pouch.

4. Submerge the pouch in the water bath and set the timer for 60 minutes.

5. When done remove from the water bath and let it cool for a few minutes. When the syrup is cool enough to handle, discard the basil leaves.

6. Empty the rest of the contents into an airtight container.

7. Refrigerate until use, for up to 10 days.

Chapter Three: Sous Vide Infusions, Canning Beans and Grains

Infused Olive Oil

Makes: 4 cups

Ingredients:

- Herbs or spices of your choice, like basil, chili, etc., for infusion

- 4 cups olive oil or any other vegetable oil of your choice

Directions:

1. Follow the instructions given in the manual and fill the sous vide water oven. Preheat it to 131°F.

2. Pour oil into a vacuum-seal pouch. Add your infusion ingredients.

3. Vacuum seal the pouch.

4. Submerge the pouch in the water bath and set the timer for 3 hours.

5. When done, remove the pouch from the water bath. Let the oil cool and strain if desired. Empty the contents into a bottle, and fasten the lid.

6. Refrigerate until use, for up to 2 months.

Infused Vinegar

Makes: About 3 cups

Ingredients:

- Zest of 2 lemons

- 2 shallots, minced

- 1 cup tarragon leaves

- 25 ounces white wine vinegar

Directions:

1. Follow the instructions given in the manual and fill the sous vide water oven. Preheat it to 135°F.

2. Add all the ingredients into a vacuum-seal pouch or Mason jar.

3. Vacuum seal the pouch or fasten the lid lightly.

4. Submerge the pouch in the water bath and set the timer for 2 hours.

5. When done, remove the pouch or jar from the water bath and let it cool. When cooled, strain into a separate jar, discarding the solids. Fasten the lid.

6. Refrigerate until use, for up to 12 days.

Grains in Canning Jars

Serves: 4

Ingredients:

- 1 cup whole grains like quinoa, steel-cut oats, or brown rice

- 1 teaspoon kosher salt

- 1 ½ cups warm water for quinoa or rice and 2 cups water for oats

Directions:

1. Follow the instructions given in the manual and fill the sous vide water oven. Preheat it to 180°F.

2. Take a large canning jar. Add your grains and water accordingly. Add salt and stir.

3. Fasten the lid lightly, but not tight at all.

4. Submerge the canning jar in water bath and adjust the timer for 3 hours.

5. When done, remove the jars from the water bath and cool completely.

6. Use as required or place in the refrigerator until use.

Sous Vide Navy Beans, With Prior Soaking

Serves: 2 or 3

Ingredients:

- 3.5 ounces dry navy beans
- ½ teaspoon salt + extra for cooking
- 18 ounces water + extra for cooking

Directions:

1. Follow the instructions given in the manual and fill the sous vide water oven. Preheat it to 194°F.

2. Add beans into a container and top with 18 ounces water. Cover and place in the refrigerator for 16 to 24 hours.

3. Remove from the refrigerator and drain. Rinse a couple of times.

4. Place beans in a vacuum-seal pouch or Ziploc bag. Add a cup of water and ½ teaspoon salt.

5. Submerge the pouch in the water bath and adjust the timer for 90 minutes. After about 80 minutes of cooking, remove the bag and press the beans (through the bag) and check if they are cooked. If the beans are cooked, switch off the water bath; if not, continue cooking until the beans are tender.

6. When the timer goes off, remove the bag from the water bath. Empty the contents from the pouch into an airtight container.

7. Refrigerate until use, for up to 4 days.

Sous Vide Beans, Without Soaking

Serves: 8

Ingredients:

- 2 cups dried pinto beans, rinsed

- 4 cloves garlic, crushed

- 2 teaspoons kosher salt

- 1 onion, halved

- 2 teaspoons dried oregano

- 6 cups water

To serve:

- Cayenne pepper

- Sour cream

Directions:

1. Follow the instructions given in the manual and fill the sous vide water oven. Preheat it to 190°F.

2. Add all the ingredients into a vacuum-seal pouch or Ziploc bag.

3. Vacuum seal the pouch.

4. Submerge the pouch in the water bath and adjust the timer for 6 hours. After about 5 hours of cooking, remove the bag and press the beans (through the bag) and check if they are

cooked. If the beans are cooked, switch off the water bath; if not, continue cooking until the beans are tender.

5. When done, remove from the water bath and let cool for a few minutes. Drain off the liquid and remove the onion and garlic.

6. Refrigerate until use, for up to 4 days.

7. To serve: Warm the beans and drizzle with sour cream. Sprinkle cayenne pepper on top and serve.

Lentils in Canning Jars

Serves: 8

Ingredients:

- 2 cups dried lentils, rinsed

- 2 teaspoons kosher salt

- Warm water as required

- 2 bay leaves

Directions:

1. Follow the instructions given in the manual and fill the sous vide water oven. Preheat it to 190°F.

2. Take a large canning jar. Add lentils. Pour warm water into the jar (fill up to the neck).

3. Add bay leaves and salt into the jar. You can use 2 jars if you do not have a large enough jar.

4. Fasten the lid lightly, but not very tight.

5. Submerge the canning jars in water bath and adjust the timer for 2 hours.

6. When done, remove the jar and cool completely.

7. Discard the bay leaves.

8. Use as required or cool completely and refrigerate until use, for up to 4 days.

Chapter Four: Breakfast Recipes

Overnight Oatmeal

Serves: 4

Ingredients:

- 2/3 cup rolled oats

- 2/3 cup pinhead oatmeal

- 1 1/3 cups milk or cream

- 4 teaspoons raisins

- 2 cups water

- 2 teaspoons maple syrup or honey

Directions:

1. Follow the instructions given in the manual and fill the sous vide water oven. Preheat it to 140°F.

2. Take 4 Mason jars or glass jam jars with lids. Divide the oats and pinhead oatmeal (you can also use quick-cook steel-cut oats) among the jars. Divide the milk and pour over the oats. Pour ½ cup water in each jar.

3. Add a teaspoon of raisins to each jar. Fasten the lids lightly, not tight.

4. Immerse the filled jars in the water bath. The lids of the jars should be above the level of water in the cooker. This is important.

5. Set the timer for 9 to 10 hours.

6. When done, stir and serve with some butter, if desired.

Overnight Oatmeal with Stewed Fruit Compote

Serves: 4

Ingredients:

<u>For oatmeal:</u>

- 2 cups quick-cooking rolled oats
- ¼ teaspoon ground cinnamon
- 6 cups water
- A pinch salt

<u>For Stewed Fruit Compote:</u>

- 1½ cups mixed dried fruit of your choice—cherries, apricots, cranberries, etc.
- 1 cup water
- Zest of an orange, finely grated
- Zest of a lemon, finely grated
- ¼ cup white sugar
- ¼ teaspoon vanilla extract

Directions:

1. Follow the instructions given in the manual and fill the sous vide water oven. Preheat it to 155°F.

2. Place oatmeal, water, salt, and cinnamon in a vacuum-seal pouch or Ziploc bag.

3. Place all the ingredients of the fruit compote in another similar pouch, and vacuum seal both.

4. Submerge both pouches in the water bath and set the timer for 6 to 10 hours.

5. Remove the pouches and shake them well.

6. Divide the oatmeal into 4 bowls. Top with fruit compote and serve.

French Toast

Serves: 8

Ingredients:

- 8 slices bread
- 1 cup heavy cream
- 1 teaspoon ground cinnamon
- 4 eggs
- 2 teaspoons vanilla extract

For finishing:

- ½ cup butter

Directions:

1. Follow the instructions given in the manual and fill the sous vide water oven. Preheat it to 147°F.

2. Add eggs, vanilla, cream, and cinnamon into a bowl and whisk well.

3. Dip the bread slices in the egg mixture, one at a time, and place in a large vacuum-seal pouch or Ziploc bag. Use 2 bags, if desired. Place in a single layer.

4. Vacuum seal the pouch.

5. Submerge the pouch in the water bath. Set the timer for 60 minutes.

6. Remove the pouch from the water bath and remove the bread slices from the pouch.

7. For finishing: Place a large skillet over medium heat.

8. Add 1 or 2 tablespoons butter. When butter melts, place 2 or 3 bread slices on the pan and cook to desired doneness.

Perfect Egg Tostada

Serves: 4

Ingredients:

- 4 large eggs, at room temperature

- ¼ cup cooked or canned black beans, heated

- 4 sprigs cilantro, chopped

- 4 corn tostadas

- 4 teaspoons salsa taquera or salsa Verde or chili de arbol

- 4 teaspoons queso fresco, crumbled

Directions:

1. Follow the instructions given in the manual and fill the sous vide water oven. Preheat it to 162°F.

2. Place the eggs on a spoon, one at a time, and gently lower them into the water bath and place on the rack. Set the timer for 15 minutes.

3. When the timer goes off, immediately remove the eggs from the water bath. Place the eggs in a bowl of cold water for a few minutes.

4. To assemble: Place the tostadas on 4 serving plates. Spread a tablespoon of beans over it, then salsa, then sprinkle cheese on top and serve.

Poached Eggs in Hash Brown Nests

Serves: 3

Ingredients:

- 6 large eggs, at room temperature
- 3 cups frozen shredded hash brown, thawed completely
- 1 teaspoon fresh rosemary, chopped, or ¼ teaspoon dried rosemary
- Freshly ground pepper to taste
- Salt to taste
- 2 tablespoons chopped fresh chives
- 1 ½ tablespoons extra-virgin olive oil
- ¼ teaspoon paprika
- 3 thin slices prosciutto, halved crosswise
- Cooking spray

Directions:

1. Follow the instructions given in the manual and fill the sous vide water oven. Preheat it to 147°F.

2. Place the eggs on a spoon, one at a time, and gently lower them into the water bath and place on the lower rack. Set the timer for 60 minutes.

3. Meanwhile, grease a 6-count muffin pan with cooking spray.

4. Place hash browns on a kitchen towel. Squeeze out as much moisture as possible.

5. Place the hash browns in a bowl. Add oil, rosemary, pepper, paprika, and salt. Mix well.

6. Divide this mixture among the muffin cups. Press down at the bottom and sides of the muffin cups. Spray cooking spray over it.

7. Preheat oven to 375°F.

8. Place the muffin tin in the oven and bake for about 30 minutes or until nearly golden brown.

9. Place half slice of prosciutto over each hash brown. Let it hang from the edges of the hash brown nests. Bake for 5 minutes.

10. Remove from the oven and cool for 4 or 5 minutes. Run a knife around the edges of the hash brown nest and gently lift it out from the muffin tin.

11. When the timer of the sous vide cooker goes off, immediately remove the eggs. Break 2 cooked eggs in each nest. Garnish with chives and serve immediately.

Egg with Sunchoke Velouté, Crispy Prosciutto and Hazelnut

Serves: 3

Ingredients:

For sunchoke velouté:

- 2 tablespoons butter
- 1 small leek, only white part, thinly sliced
- 1 pound Jerusalem artichokes (sunchokes), peeled, sliced
- ½ quart milk
- ¼ cup heavy cream (optional)
- 1 medium onion, thinly sliced
- 1 clove garlic, sliced
- ½ quart chicken stock
- ¼ vanilla bean, scraped

For bouquet garni:

- 2 or 3 thyme sprigs
- 2 or 3 fresh sage leaves
- 1 bay leaf
- Leek greens, to wrap

For sous vide eggs:

- 3 eggs, at room temperature

For finishing:

- 3 thin slices prosciutto

- Few strips fried Jerusalem artichokes (sunchokes)

- A handful baby watercress

- 6 hazelnuts, toasted, chopped

- Oil, as required

Directions:

1. Follow the instructions given in the manual and fill the sous vide water oven. Preheat it to 145°F.

2. Place the eggs on a spoon and gently lower them into the water bath. Place on the lower rack. Set the timer for 47 minutes.

3. Meanwhile, make the sunchoke velouté as follows: Place a casserole dish over medium flame. Add butter. When butter melts, add onion, garlic, leeks, salt and pepper.

4. To make bouquet garni, place together thyme, sage, and bay leaf and wrap it with leek greens.

5. Place bouquet garni in the casserole dish. Cook for a few minutes.

6. Stir in the artichokes and cook until slightly tender. Stir occasionally.

7. Add rest of the ingredients and stir. Once it boils, reduce the flame and let it simmer until tender. Turn off the heat and remove the bouquet garni.

8. Blend the mixture in a blender. Strain the mixture through a wire mesh strainer placed over a saucepan.

9. To finish: Smear oil over the prosciutto slices and lay them on a lined baking sheet.

10. Bake in a preheated oven at 300°F until crisp. Remove from the oven and cool.

11. Place a few strips of sunchoke on a nonstick pan. Add a bit of oil. Add sunchoke and cook until crisp. Sprinkle salt.

12. Crack a cooked egg into each of 3 bowls.

13. Spoon the sunchoke velouté over the eggs in each bowl.

14. Serve topped with prosciutto, hazelnuts, watercress, and fried sunchoke strips.

Sausage Scramble

Serves: 3

Ingredients:

- 16 large eggs, well beaten

- 8 ounces breakfast sausages, crumbled

- 4 tablespoons butter

- Salt and pepper, as per taste

- ½ cup Mexican cheese, grated

Directions:

1. Follow the instructions given in the manual and fill the sous vide water oven. Preheat it to 165°F.

2. Place a skillet over medium heat and cook the sausages until they are browned.

3. Transfer the cooked sausages in a bowl lined with paper towels and allow them to cool. Once the sausages cool, place them in a Ziploc bag. Add the eggs, butter, cheese, salt and pepper and vacuum seal the bag.

4. Submerge and cook in the sous vide cooker for around 20 minutes. Take the pouch out occasionally and shake the contents well before submerging again. Cook until the eggs are as per your liking.

5. Remove from the water bath and serve.

Eggs Benedict

Serves: 4

Ingredients:

- 4 English muffins, halved, toasted

- 8 slices Canadian bacon

- A handful fresh parsley, chopped

- 8 eggs

- Butter, as required

For hollandaise sauce:

- 8 tablespoons butter

- 2 teaspoons lemon juice

- 1 shallot, diced

- Salt to taste

- Cayenne pepper to taste

- 2 egg yolks

- 2 teaspoons water

Directions:

1. Follow the instructions given in the manual and fill the sous vide water oven. Preheat it to 148°F.

2. Place the eggs in a vacuum-seal pouch or Ziploc bag. Place all the ingredients for hollandaise sauce into another bag. Vacuum seal the pouches.

3. Submerge both pouches in the water bath and set the timer for 1 hour.

4. Meanwhile, cook the bacon in a pan to the desired doneness. Keep warm in an oven along with muffins if desired.

5. Remove the pouches from the water bath. Transfer the contents of the sauce into a blender and blend until smooth.

6. Place muffins on individual serving plates. Crack an egg on each muffin and place on the bottom half of the muffins.

7. Spoon hollandaise over the eggs and garnish with parsley. Cover with the top half of the muffins and serve.

Smoked Fish and Poached Egg

Serves: 4

Ingredients:

- 4 fillets smoked fish
- 2 lemons, cut into slices
- Seasonings of your choice
- 4 large eggs
- 4 tablespoons olive oil

Directions:

1. Follow the instructions given in the manual and fill the sous vide water oven. Preheat it to 140°F.

2. Divide all the ingredients except eggs into 4 vacuum-seal pouches or Ziploc bags.

3. Seal the pouches, but do not remove the air completely.

4. Submerge both pouches in the water bath and set the timer for 20 minutes.

5. When the timer goes off, remove the pouches and set aside.

6. Increase the temperature to 167°F.

7. Place the eggs on a spoon, one at a time, and gently lower them into the water bath and place on the lower rack. Set the timer for 15 minutes.

8. Empty each pouch onto individual serving plates. Break an egg over each fillet and serve.

Brioche and Eggs

Serves: 6

Ingredients:

- 6 brioche buns

- 6 large eggs

- 2 scallions, sliced (optional)

- 1 ½ cups grated cheese

Directions:

1. Follow the instructions given in the manual and fill the sous vide water oven. Preheat it to 149°F.

2. Place the eggs on a spoon, one at a time, and gently lower them into the water bath and place on the rack. Set the timer for 45 minutes.

3. When the timer goes off, immediately remove the eggs from the water bath. Place the eggs in a bowl of cold water for a few minutes.

4. Place brioche buns on a baking sheet and break a cooked egg on each bun. Sprinkle cheese on top.

5. Set an oven to broil and place the baking sheet in the oven. Broil for few minutes until cheese melts.

Egg Bites

Serves: 4

Ingredients:

- 5 eggs
- ¼ cup shredded Colby Jack cheese
- 3 tablespoons unsweetened almond milk
- Salt to taste
- Pepper to taste

Directions:

1. Follow the instructions given in the manual and fill the sous vide water oven. Preheat it to 172°F.

2. Add a tablespoon of cheese into each of 4 canning jars or Mason jars.

3. Whisk together eggs and milk in a bowl. Divide the egg mixture among the jars. Season with salt and pepper.

4. Fasten the lid lightly, not very tight.

5. Submerge the canning jars in water bath and adjust the timer for 1 hour or until eggs are set.

6. Remove the jars from the water bath. Serve directly from the jars.

Sous Vide Scrambled Eggs

Serves: 4

Ingredients:

- 8 large eggs
- Freshly ground pepper to taste
- Salt to taste
- Aleppo pepper to taste (optional)
- 2 tablespoons butter

Directions:

1. Follow the instructions given in the manual and fill the sous vide water oven. Preheat it to 165°F.
2. Add eggs, salt, and pepper into a bowl and whisk well. Pour into a large silicone bag and vacuum seal the pouch.
3. Submerge the pouch in the water bath and adjust the timer for 10 minutes.
4. Remove the pouch from the water bath and place the pouch between your palms. Press it and shake it.
5. Place it back in the water bath. Set the timer for 12 minutes.
6. When the timer goes off, remove the pouch from the water bath.
7. Open the pouch and divide onto 4 plates.
8. Garnish with Aleppo pepper. Serve immediately.

Cured Salmon

Serves: 2

Ingredients:

- 2 salmon fillets (6 ounces each)
- 8 tablespoons sugar
- 8 tablespoons salt
- 2 teaspoons smoke flavor powder (optional)

Directions:

1. Take 2 bowls and place a fillet in each bowl.
2. Divide the sugar, salt and smoke flavor powder among the bowls. Mix well. Set aside for 30 minutes.
3. Rinse the fillets in water.
4. Place in a large Ziploc bag. Vacuum seal the pouch.
5. Submerge the pouch in the water bath and adjust the timer for 30 minutes.
6. Just before the timer goes off, make an ice water bath by filling a large bowl with water and ice.
7. When done, remove the pouch from the water bath and immerse in the ice water bath. When cooled, remove the pouch from the water bath.
8. Remove the fillets from the pouch and serve.

Chapter Five: Sous Vide Soup Recipes

Split Lentil Soup with Smoked Ham Hock

Serves: 4

Ingredients:

- 5 cups chicken stock

- 2 smoked ham hocks

- 1 cup finely diced carrot

- 1 cup finely diced celery

- ½ cup finely diced onions

- 2 cups split lentils

- Freshly ground pepper to taste

- Kosher salt to taste

- 2 bay leaves

Directions:

1. Follow the instructions given in the manual and fill the sous vide water oven. Preheat it to 180°F.

2. Add all the ingredients into a large vacuum-seal pouch or Ziploc bag.

3. Vacuum seal the pouch.

4. Submerge the pouch in the water bath. Set the timer for 2 hours.

5. For finishing: Remove the pouch from the water bath and throw out the bay leaves.

6. Take out the ham hock. Remove and discard the bones and fat.

7. Add rest of the ingredients of the pouch into a blender and blend until smooth.

8. Pour into bowls. Divide the meat among the bowls and serve.

Creamy Celery Soup

Serves: 3

Ingredients:

- ½ cup heavy cream
- 2 cups celery, diced roughly
- ½ cup russet potatoes, peeled, diced into small squares
- ½ cup stock (vegetable or chicken)
- ½ cup leek, diced into large pieces
- 1 tablespoon butter
- 1 bay leaf
- 1 teaspoon kosher salt or to taste
- White pepper powder to taste

Directions:

1. Follow the instructions given in the manual and fill the sous vide water oven. Preheat it to 180°F.

2. Toss all ingredients in a Ziploc bag and vacuum seal it. Submerge it in a water bath for about an hour, or until the vegetables are cooked.

3. Once all the ingredients are cooked, take out the bay leaf and puree the rest of the ingredients. Strain the contents through a strainer or sieve discard the remaining solids. Serve hot.

Chicken Ramen

Serves: 4

Ingredients:

- 1 pound chicken thighs, skinless, boneless
- 4 cloves garlic, peeled, minced
- 2 medium onions, chopped
- 4 carrots, peeled, thinly sliced
- 1 medium head Chinese cabbage, shredded
- 2 tablespoons tomato paste
- 8 cups chicken stock
- 2 tablespoons tomato paste
- 4 tablespoons grated fresh ginger
- 4 tablespoons Japanese soy sauce
- 2 tablespoons oil
- 2 tablespoons sugar
- Shichimi togarashi or plain red pepper flakes to taste
- 2 bay leaves
- 2 star anise
- 7 ounces ramen or any other oriental noodles
- 2 scallions, thinly sliced

Directions:

1. Follow the instructions given in the manual and fill the sous vide water oven. Preheat it to 144°F.

2. Place a skillet over medium heat and add oil. When the oil is heated, add onions, garlic, shichimi, and 2 tablespoons ginger. Sauté until the onions are translucent.

3. Add tomato paste and mix well. Remove from heat. Add chicken, carrots, stock, soy sauce, star anise, sugar, and bay leaves. Mix well.

4. Transfer into a large Ziploc bag or vacuum-seal pouch.

5. Submerge the pouch in the water bath and adjust the timer for 8 to 10 hours, or until the chicken is cooked.

6. Remove the chicken from the pouch and, once cool enough to handle, shred the chicken and set it aside. Add rest of the ingredients of the pouch into a pot.

7. Place the pot over medium heat. Add noodles and cabbage and cook until the noodles are al dente.

8. Discard star anise and bay leaves. Add chicken and 2 tablespoons ginger. Heat thoroughly.

9. Serve in bowls. Garnish with green onions and serve.

Chicken and Vegetable Soup

Serves: 8

Ingredients:

- 2 cups zucchini, diced

- 2 cups cauliflower, chopped

- 2 cups red bell pepper, diced

- 8 cups fresh spinach leaves

- 12 baby carrots, chopped

- 2 large onions, chopped

- 2 teaspoons of garlic powder or to taste

- Cayenne pepper to taste

- 4 cups chicken, diced, sous vide cooked

- 8 cups chicken broth

- 2 teaspoons onion powder

- Sea salt to taste

- Black pepper powder to taste

- 2 tablespoons olive oil

Directions:

1. Follow the instructions given in the manual and fill the sous vide water oven. Preheat it to 180°F.

2. Place all the vegetables in a bowl and add all the spices into another bowl. Mix well, then sprinkle the spice mixture over the vegetables. Toss well and transfer into a large Ziploc bag or a vacuum-seal pouch and vacuum seal it. Submerge the pouch in the water bath and adjust the timer for 1 hour, or until the vegetables are cooked.

3. To make the soup: Place a soup pot over medium heat and add oil. When the oil is heated, add broth and let it come to a boil.

4. Lower heat, empty the contents of the pouch into the pot and add chicken and stir. Simmer for 5 to 7 minutes. Turn off the heat.

5. Serve in soup bowls. Serve hot.

Wild Mushroom Bisque

Serves: 8

Ingredients:

- 2 pounds assorted wild mushrooms of your choice
- 2 shallots, thinly sliced
- 4 tablespoons brandy or cognac
- Salt to taste
- Freshly ground pepper to taste
- 1 cup heavy cream
- 6 tablespoons unsalted butter
- 2 tablespoons minced, fresh thyme
- 2 cloves garlic, peeled, minced
- 4 cups water
- Olive oil, to drizzle (optional)

Directions:

1. Follow the instructions given in the manual and fill the sous vide water oven. Preheat it to 190°F.

2. Add all the ingredients into a large vacuum-seal pouch or Ziploc bag.

3. Vacuum seal the pouch.

4. Submerge the pouch in the water bath. Set the timer for 1 hour.

5. When the timer goes off, remove pouch from the water bath. Transfer into a blender and blend until smooth.

6. Serve in bowls. Trickle oil on top, if using, and serve.

Tomato Soup

Serves: 5 to 7

Ingredients:

- 1 can whole or diced tomatoes, peeled
- 1 small fresh tomato, chopped
- 1 small green pepper, chopped
- 1 tablespoon flour
- A pinch cayenne pepper
- 1 tablespoon dried basil leaves
- ¼ cup heavy cream

- ¼ cup butter

- 1 cup milk

- 1 clove garlic, chopped

- Salt and pepper, as needed

Direction:

1. Heat a saucepan over medium flame and melt half the butter. Add the flour and sauté for a couple of minutes until it becomes brown. Make sure you stir it constantly.

2. Add the milk and continue stirring until the mixture starts bubbling and thickens.

3. Pour the cream and stir again for a minute. Don't let it boil—once it's warm enough, take it off the heat and set aside.

4. Heat another saucepan over medium flame. Melt the rest of the butter and add onions, garlic, and green pepper. Sauté for 3 to 4 minutes.

5. Add diced tomatoes, chopped tomato, and basil and mix well.

6. Reduce the heat and add cayenne pepper, white sauce, salt and pepper.

7. Follow the instructions given in the manual and fill the sous vide water oven. Preheat it to 175°F.

8. Transfer the vegetables to a Ziploc bag and vacuum seal it. Submerge the pouch in the water bath for 45 minutes.

9. When cooked, puree the soup and serve hot.

Beet Soup with Caraway and Yogurt

Serves: 8

Ingredients:

- 2 tablespoons extra-virgin olive oil

- 2 medium onions, chopped

- Salt to taste

- 2 bay leaves

- 1 cup whole milk yogurt + extra to serve

- Fresh dill fronds, to serve

- 3 teaspoons caraway seeds

- 2 leeks, halved, thinly sliced

- 4 pounds beets, peeled, chopped

- 6 cups chicken broth or water

- 1 tablespoon apple cider vinegar or to taste

Directions:

1. Follow the instructions given in the manual and fill the sous vide water oven. Preheat it to 185°F.

2. Place a skillet over medium flame and add oil. When the oil is heated, add caraway seeds. When they crackle, add leeks, onion and a bit of salt and cook until tender. Turn off the heat.

3. Add beets, about a teaspoon of salt, and bay leaves and mix well. Transfer into 2 large vacuum-seal pouches or Ziploc bags.

4. Vacuum seal the pouches.

5. Submerge the pouches in the water bath. Set the timer for 2 hours.

6. When the timer goes off, remove pouch from the water bath. Transfer into a blender. Add some broth and blend until smooth.

7. Pour into a saucepan. Add yogurt, vinegar, and salt to taste. Mix well.

8. Serve in bowls and drizzle some yogurt on top. Place dill fronds in each bowl and serve.

Sweet Corn and Green Chili Soup

Serves: 8

Ingredients:

- 2 bags frozen sweet corn

- 6 bulbs roasted garlic, peeled

- 2 cups chicken stock

- 1 medium onion, sautéed to golden brown

- Salt to taste

- Pepper to taste

- 2 large whole green chilies, char the skin using a culinary torch, deseed if desired

Directions:

1. Follow the instructions given in the manual and fill the sous vide water oven. Preheat it to 83°F.

2. Add all the ingredients except green chilies into a large vacuum-seal pouch or Ziploc bag.

3. Vacuum seal the pouch.

4. Submerge the pouch in the water bath. Set the timer for 1½ hours or until cooked.

5. When the timer goes off, remove pouch from the water bath. Transfer into a blender. Add the green chilies and blend until smooth.

6. Strain the soup if desired. Taste and adjust the seasonings if required.

7. Serve in bowls.

Tri Tip Chili

Serves: 8

Ingredients:

- 4 pounds tri tip roast

- 2 onions, diced

- 2 cans (15 ounces each) petite diced tomatoes, with its juices

- 4 tablespoons tomato paste

- 16 ounces tomato sauce (refer to chapter on sauces for the recipe)

- 3 cups beef broth

- 2 tablespoons olive oil

- 2 cans (15.5 ounces each) red kidney beans, drained, rinsed

- 4 tablespoons ground cumin

- 2 tablespoons garlic powder

- 1 teaspoon pepper, or to taste

- 5 tablespoons chili powder, or to taste

- 3 tablespoons sugar

- 2 teaspoons salt, or to taste

- ½ teaspoon cayenne pepper

To serve:

- Sour cream

- Grated cheddar cheese

Directions:

1. Follow the instructions given in the manual and fill the sous vide water oven. Preheat it to 131°F.

2. Sprinkle salt over the tri tip and place in a large vacuum bag. Vacuum seal the pouch.

3. Submerge the pouch in the water bath. Set the timer for 3 hours or until cooked.

4. When the timer goes off, remove pouch from the water bath. Remove the tri tip from the pouch and dry by patting with paper towels.

5. Place a large skillet over high heat. Add oil and let it heat.

6. Sprinkle salt and pepper over the meat and place in the pan. Cook for a couple of minutes. Flip and cook well on the other side, too.

7. Remove meat and, when it is cool enough to handle, cut into bite-sized pieces. Set it aside.

8. To make chili: Place a large soup pot over medium heat and add oil. When the oil is heated, onions and sauté until translucent.

9. Add all the spices, sugar, and tomato paste and stir for a few seconds until aromatic.

10. Stir in broth, beans, tomatoes, and tomato sauce. When it begins to boil, reduce the heat and simmer for about 30 minutes. Stir every 10 minutes. Turn off the heat.

11. Cover the pot. Let the chili sit for 10 minutes. Add the tri tip meat into the pot and stir.

12. Serve in bowls. Garnish with cheddar cheese and sour cream.

Borscht

Serves: 4

Ingredients:

- 2 large beetroots, peeled, sliced
- 1 medium onion, peeled, sliced
- ¼ head red cabbage, thinly sliced
- ½ cup chopped dill + extra to serve
- Salt to taste
- Pepper to taste

- 2 large carrots, peeled, sliced

- 1 medium russet potato, peeled, sliced

- 4 cups vegetable broth or beef broth

- 1 ½ tablespoons red wine vinegar

- ½ cup sour cream, to serve

Directions:

1. Follow the instructions given in the manual and fill the sous vide water oven. Preheat it to 83°F.

2. Add carrots, beets, potato, and onions in a single into a large vacuum-seal pouch or Ziploc bag.

3. Add cabbage in another pouch.

4. Vacuum seal the pouches.

5. Submerge the pouches in the water bath. Set the timer for 1½ hours or until vegetables are cooked.

6. When the timer goes off, remove pouches from the water bath. Transfer the contents of beets pouch into a blender and blend until smooth.

7. Taste and adjust the seasonings if required.

8. Place a soup pot over high heat and let it come to a boil. Add blended soup, cabbage, vinegar, salt, pepper, and dill. Stir well and lower heat to low heat. Let it simmer for a few minutes.

9. Dish into bowls and drizzle with sour cream. Sprinkle dill on top and serve.

Beef Bourguignon

Serves: 8

Ingredients:

- 2 tablespoons extra-virgin olive oil

- 3 pounds beef chuck roast, cut into 1-inch pieces

- 3 teaspoons kosher salt, divided

- 4 carrots, quartered lengthwise, cut into 1-inch pieces

- 4 cloves garlic, peeled, minced

- 2 cups water

- 2 tablespoons tomato paste

- 2 bay leaves

- 20 ounces cremini mushrooms, thinly sliced

- 12 ounces bacon, thinly sliced into lardons

- 4 tablespoons cornstarch

- 1 teaspoon freshly ground pepper

- 2 onions, sliced

- 2 bottles dry red wine

- 2 tablespoons beef bouillon

- 2 teaspoons minced fresh thyme leaves

- 8 tablespoons unsalted butter, at room temperature, divided

- 4 tablespoons all-purpose flour

Directions:

1. Follow the instructions given in the manual and fill the sous vide water oven. Preheat it to 140°F.

2. Place a large skillet over medium heat and add oil. When the oil is heated, add bacon and cook until crisp. Remove bacon and place in a large Ziploc bag or vacuum-seal pouch.

3. Dry the beef with paper towels. Sprinkle cornstarch, pepper, and 2 teaspoons salt over the beef. Toss well.

4. Place a large pan over medium heat. Add a little of the oil. When the oil is heated, add some of the beef and cook until brown all over. Cook the remaining beef in batches, using a little of the oil with each batch.

5. Remove with a slotted spoon and place in the pouch along with bacon.

6. Add onions, carrot, and 1 teaspoon salt into the same skillet. Sauté until onions turn light brown.

7. Stir in the garlic and cook until aromatic. Turn off the heat and add the vegetables into the pouch with beef. Drain off any fat remaining in the pan.

8. Pour wine into the skillet.

9. Stir in water and beef bouillon. Cook until the liquid in the pan is reduced to ¼ its original quantity.

10. Pour into the pouch. Also add the tomato paste, bay leaves, and thyme.

11. Vacuum seal the pouch.

12. Submerge the pouch in the water bath. Set the timer for 16 to 24 hours. Use plastic wrap to cover the water bath. This helps to reduce water evaporation.

13. During the last 5 minutes of cooking, place a large skillet over medium heat and add 4 tablespoons butter. When butter melts, add mushrooms and cook until soft.

14. Remove the pouch from the water bath. Snip off a corner of the bag and add the liquid from the bag into the skillet.

15. Add 4 tablespoons butter and flour into a bowl and mix well. Add into the skillet. Increase the heat to medium-high and stir often until the sauce thickens.

16. Add meat and vegetables from the pouch into the skillet. Mix well.

17. Turn off the heat. Place in a serving bowl and sprinkle with thyme.

18. Serve with roasted potatoes or bread or mashed cauliflower, if desired.

Beef Burgundy Stew

Serves: 12

Ingredients:

- 6 slices thick-cut bacon, cut into ¼-inch strips
- 4 pounds sirloin roast, cut into 1-inch cubes
- 2 medium onions, thinly sliced
- 4 cups dry red wine
- 2 tablespoons tomato paste
- 2 cloves garlic, minced
- 2 bay leaves
- 14 ounces frozen pearl onions, thawed
- 4 tablespoons unsalted butter
- 4 carrots, peeled, cut into ¼-inch thick slices
- 6 tablespoons flour
- 3 cups beef stock
- 2 tablespoons Worcestershire sauce
- 2 teaspoons dried thyme
- 20 ounces white mushrooms, cleaned, quartered
- A handful fresh parsley, chopped, to garnish

Directions:

1. Follow the instructions given in the manual and fill the sous vide water oven. Preheat it to 140°F.

2. Place a large heavy-bottomed skillet over medium-high heat. When the pan is warm, add bacon and cook until crisp. Remove bacon and place on a plate lined with paper towels.

3. Retain about 2 tablespoons of the bacon fat (released in the pan while cooking) and discard the rest.

4. Dry the meat cubes with paper towels.

5. Add 2 tablespoons butter into the skillet. When butter melts, add meat in a single layer and cook until brown all over. Cook in batches if required.

6. Stir in the carrots and onion and cook until slightly tender.

7. Sprinkle flour on top and mix until the meat and vegetables are well coated.

8. Pour wine into the skillet, then stir in 2 cups stock, Worcestershire sauce, bay leaves, tomato paste, garlic and thyme and mix well.

9. When it begins to boil, lower heat and cook until slightly thick. Turn off the heat.

10. Transfer into 1 or 2 large vacuum-seal pouches or Ziploc bags. Vacuum seal the pouches.

11. Submerge the pouch in the water bath. Adjust the timer for 6 hours.

12. During the last 30 minutes of cooking, place a skillet over medium heat and add 2 tablespoons butter. When butter melts, add mushroom and pearl onions and cook until dry.

13. Stir in rest of the stock and cook until dry. Remove the mushrooms into a large bowl.

14. To finish: Place a fine wire mesh strainer over a bowl. Empty the pouch into the strainer and add the solids into the bowl of mushrooms.

15. Pour the strained liquid into a skillet. Place the skillet over medium flame and let it come to a boil. Discard any scum and fat that is floating on top. Reduce the heat and simmer until slightly thick.

16. Stir in the meat and mushroom mixture. Mix well. Heat thoroughly. Transfer into a bowl.

17. Sprinkle parsley on top and serve.

Chapter Six: About the Wagyu Breed

About the Wagyu Breed

Wagyu is a type of Japanese cattle breed native to Asia. The term Wagyu literally translates to "Japanese cow." These animals were used in agriculture as draft animals and they were chosen because of their physical endurance. These animals were favored because they had more intramuscular fat cells, which provided their body with a readily available source of energy. Wagyu breed has horns, and the cattle are either red or black.

History of the Breed

Research shows that there was some separation in the genes in cattle almost 35,000 years ago, which led to the formation of the Wagyu genetic strain. The Wagyu cattle available today are a result of the crossing of imported breeds with the native cattle in Japan. When the government decided to introduce the Western culture and food habits, Japan imported Brown Swiss, Simmental, Devon, Korean, Ayrshire and Shorthorn cattle. In the year 1910, the infusion of the Asian, British, and European breeds were cut off from outside infusions with other genes.

Four breeds in Japan are considered to have Wagyu strains. These are:

- Japanese Brown, also termed as Red Wagyu in the US

- Japanese Black, the Wagyu breed that is often exported to the US

- Japanese Shorthorn

- Japanese Polled

Japanese Shorthorn or Japanese Polled are not bred in any other parts of the world.

History of the Breed in the US

It was in the year 1975 that Japan first exported the Wagyu breed to the US. Two red and two black bulls were imported to Morris Whitney. The Japanese reduced the tariffs that they imposed on imported beef in the year 1989. This finally encouraged the producers in the US to work on producing a high-quality product for Japan. There were several high qualities of Wagyu imported from Japan to the US in the year 1990. Most of these imported Wagyu were black, and the remainder was red. The producers in the US decided to crossbreed and hence Wagyu had a great influence on the herds here and most other countries across the globe.

Wagyu in the US Today

The American Wagyu Association was set up in Texas in March 1990. This association serves as the registry of the Wagyu cattle in Canada, the US and other countries. The headquarters of this association is in Post Falls. This association promotes and develops a sustainable Wagyu industry in the US. Wagyu beef can offer numerous opportunities. This industry caters to the feeders and breeders. It also targets the high-end restaurants and connects these restaurants with the best producers. The quality of red meat has increased in the US because of the Wagyu breed.

Healthy and Delicious Wagyu Beef

There is no other form of beef that is as tender and tasty as the Wagyu beef. It is for this reason that many gourmet cooks, restaurants and homes across the US seek out and consume Wagyu beef when available. This meat is a gastronomic delight, and it is extremely healthy for you too. The ratio of the saturated to monounsaturated fat is higher in Wagyu when compared to other types of beef. The saturated fat in Wagyu is composed differently as compared to those fats in other types of beef. Stearic acid contains forty percent of the saturated fat in Wagyu beef, but this acid has minimal or no impact on the cholesterol levels in the body, which makes this beef healthier and beneficial to human health.

Wagyu also contains large quantities of conjugated linoleic acid (CLA). This beef has 30% more CLA when compared to other breeds of beef. Foods that have a higher proportion of CLA will have less of a negative effect on health.

Using Sous Vide to Cook Wagyu

Wagyu meat will melt in your mouth if you cook it well. This is also, however, the most expensive kind of beef in the world. So, if you are spending a lot of money on buying the beef, you need to know how to cook it well too. If you are someone who loves to eat Wagyu and are a sous vide enthusiast, you are probably wondering if you can cook Wagyu beef using the sous vide technique.

There are many options: You can cook beef over an open fire either with or without charcoal, straight on a cast iron pan, cook a steak tartare, slice the beef thin or into cubes and cook it, eat it as a 1.5-inch steak or even use the sous vide technique.

Some people are afraid to use this technique to cook Wagyu meat. And you must be wondering if you can? Wouldn't it be better just to sear the meat on a pan? To answer the previous question, yes, you can use the sous vide technique to cook Wagyu. Do you worry because this technique might make the fat melt? Well, it won't. It is important to remember that you can either under or overcook the meat when you sear it on a pan.

The sous vide technique will offer a lot more precision. You can set the temperature to 129 degrees Fahrenheit and know the meat is fully cooked. The fat will be heated and cooked to a texture that will melt in your mouth. You will be sure that the meat is not under or overcooked. So, ignore the chatter about how you should not sous vide Wagyu meat. Be confident that you can reduce your chances of messing up the meat and cook this steak to perfection every time. It is easier to cook Wagyu using the sous vide technique as all you need to do is set the temperature, pop the meat into the machine and watch magic happen as you impress your dinner guests

Chapter Seven: Wagyu Recipes

Wagyu Sous Vide

Servings: 6 to 8

Ingredients:

- Wagyu fillet

- 1 sprig of rosemary

- Salt to taste

- Pepper to taste

Directions:

1. Take a large pot and place the sous vide in the pot. Pour enough water, so that it crosses the minimum line in the sous vide machine.

2. If you want to cook the meat rare, set the temperature to 120 degrees Fahrenheit. You can look at the other temperatures you can consider at the end of the chapter.

3. Rub the fillet with salt and pepper. Place the fillet in a vacuum-sealed bag. Add the sprig of rosemary to the bag, and seal it.

4. When the temperature in the machine reaches 125 degrees Fahrenheit, drop the bag into the machine.

5. Cook the meat for 45 minutes. It is okay if you forget to pull the meat out in 45 minutes. The temperature of the meat will not exceed the temperature you set in the machine.

6. Place a skillet on medium flame and add olive oil to it. When the Wagyu is done, place the skillet on the pan and cook the meat. Cook on each side for one minute.

7. Cut into slices and serve hot.

Wagyu Steak

Servings: 2 to 6

Ingredients:

- 1 Wagyu steak (1 inch thick)

- 1 clove garlic

- 1 tbsp extra virgin olive oil

- 1 green onion, finely chopped

- 1 tbsp olive oil for searing

- 1 tbsp ponzu

- 2.5 cm daikon radish

- Salt and pepper, as needed

Directions:

1. Place the sous vide machine in a large pot and fill it with water. Make sure to exceed the minimum line inside the machine.

2. Heat the water until it reaches the required temperature. Please review the temperature from the list below.

3. Slice the clove of garlic.

4. While the water heats, remove the excess fat from the Wagyu steak. Rub the steak with salt and pepper. If you are using a vacuum bag, you can place the steak inside the bag. If you are using a food saver pack, seal one end of the pack.

5. Transfer the steak into the bag and add the slices of garlic. Add a tablespoon of olive oil to the steak. Seal the top of the bag and place it inside the machine.

6. Choose the "moisture" button on the machine.

7. Cook the meat for 60 minutes.

8. While the steak is cooking, grate the daikon and set it aside. Squeeze the daikon and make sure to remove all the liquid.

9. When the steak is done, remove the bag from the machine. Place the steak on a paper towel to remove any extra

moisture. You need to do this if you want the steak to have a nice sear.

10. Since the steak was cooked with the garlic, it has a nice aroma and flavor. Remove the garlic slices from the steak. You must remember to never over season the meat since it will absorb the seasoning that you cook it with.

11. Place a pan on medium flame and add oil to it. When the oil is hot, add the steak to the pan and cook it on both sides. You need to cook each side of the steak for at least one minute, so that the steak has a golden-brown crust. If you want a sear mark on the steak, you need to press it down on the map. Do not move the steak in the pan. Flip the steak and repeat the same process. If you want, you can also use a grill to sear the steak.

12. Transfer the steak onto a plate and cut it into slices of ½ an inch. You do not have to worry about letting the meat rest when you use the sous vide technique to cook it.

13. Add a generous amount of grated daikon to the meat and sprinkle the green onion. Pour the ponzu over the steak. If you want, you can serve the steak with some ponzu on the side.

14. If you do not want to eat the meat immediately, you can soak the vacuum bag in ice and then place it in the refrigerator. You can enjoy the meat later.

You can set the temperature in the sous vide machine depending on how you like your meat cooked:

- Rare: 120 degrees Fahrenheit

- Medium rare: 130 degrees Fahrenheit

- Medium: 140 degrees Fahrenheit

- Medium well: 150 degrees Fahrenheit

- Well done: 160 degrees Fahrenheit

Wagyu Brisket with Barbecue Sauce

Servings: 5 to 8

Ingredients:

- 4 pounds Wagyu brisket (preferably Lone Mountain)

- Dry rub (use the ingredients that follow this list)

- tbsp butter, for finishing

- sprigs, for finishing

For the dry rub

- tbsp brown sugar

- tbsp granulated sugar

- 1 ½ tsp chili powder

- tsp garlic powder

- 1 ½ tsp cumin

- 1 ½ tsp paprika

- 1 tsp onion powder

- salt and pepper, to taste

Directions:

1. Place a sous vide machine in a cooking pot and add water to it. Pour the water until the minimum line in the machine.

2. Heat the water to 132 degrees Fahrenheit.

3. While the water heats, combine the ingredients for the dry rub in a bowl and mix them well. You can either rub the entire mixture or store the excess in a container for later.

4. If the brisket is too big, you should slice it into smaller pieces that you can put into the pouch with ease.

5. Rub each piece of the brisket with the seasoning on both sides and put the pieces into a separate vacuum sealed bag. Place the bags in the refrigerator for three hours to let the pieces marinate.

6. Add the sealed pouches to the sous vide machine and cook the meat for 48 hours.

7. Once the pieces are cooked, place a skillet on medium heat. Now, remove the pieces of the brisket from the bags and pat the pieces dry.

8. Place each piece on the pan and cook one side for a minute.

9. Add butter to the pan, and let the meat baste in the butter for a few minutes.

10. Slice the brisket and serve it hot with your favorite sides.

    You can set the temperature in the sous vide machine depending on how you like your meat:

    • Rare: 120 degrees Fahrenheit

- Medium rare: 130 degrees Fahrenheit

- Medium: 140 degrees Fahrenheit

- Medium well: 150 degrees Fahrenheit

- Well done: 160 degrees Fahrenheit

CPSIA information can be obtained
at www.ICGtesting.com
Printed in the USA
LVHW011702220221
679517LV00003B/55

9 781801 235822